NEXUS

For Solo Trumpet, Winds, and Percussion

Solo Trumpet with Piano Reduction

By JAMES CURNOW

7777 W. BLUEMOUND RD. P.O. BOX 13819 MILWAUKEE, WI 53213

PROGRAM NOTES

For Alfred Watkins, master teacher and musician, with deep appreciation for more than 38 years in music education, commissioned lovingly by his former students, colleagues, band parents, and friends.

Nexus is defined as a tie or a link between people, events and situations.

Nexus, for Solo Trumpet, Winds, and Percussion, includes several links between the composer and Alfred Watkins. Christopher Watkins, Alfred's son (Trumpet/United States Army Band "Pershing's own," Washington, D.C.) was the soloist at the premier performance with the University of Alabama at Birmingham Wind Ensemble, Dr. Susan Samuels, conductor. The composer draws upon one of his own well-known melodies, "Ballad" from *Tone Studies for Band* (written and dedicated to Alfred), to form a solid link or tie between two friends, Jim Curnow and Alfred Watkins, in one unified composition.

PERFORMANCE NOTES

The opening theme (Allegro moderato, energico), first stated in the accompaniment, is developed into a quick and agile scherzo when the soloist enters. The scherzo has two parts; one energetic and fast paced and the second more lyrical and expressive, yet the tempo remains constant.

In the slow and expressive section (Moderato e espressivo) there are two new settings of "Ballad"; one featuring the soloist and the other featuring a melodic interpretation in just the piano accompaniment.

After a brief cadenza, the scherzo returns (recapitulation) with new material being stated by the soloist against the rapid and fiery accompaniment. This leads to the finale where the trumpet states a long and sustained version of the scherzo theme while the accompaniment is rhythmic and accented.

ABOUT THE COMPOSER

American composer James Curnow received a Bachelor of Music degree from Wayne State University and a Master of Music from Michigan State University. He has taught all areas and levels of instrumental music and has received numerous awards for teaching and composition: the Outstanding Educator of America (1974), the Citation of Excellence from the National Bandmasters Association (1980), the Volkwein Award (1977 & 1979), the American Bandmasters Association Ostwald Award (1980 & 1984), the International Competition for Original Compositions for Band (1985) and the Coup de Vents Composition Competition of Le Havre, France (1994). He was named Composer of the Year (1997) by the Kentucky Music Teachers Association and the National Music Teachers Association. He has received annual ASCAP standard awards since 1979.

Curnow has been commissioned to write over 400 hundred works for concert band, brass band, orchestra, choir and various vocal and instrumental ensembles. His published works now number well over 800 hundred. As a conductor, composer and clinician, Curnow has traveled throughout the United States, Canada, Australia, Japan and Europe where his music has received wide acclaim.

Curnow currently resides in Lexington, Kentucky, and is a full time composer of commissions world-wide and publishes with Hal Leonard Corporation/Curnow Music Press, Inc. He also serves as Composer-in-Residence Emeritus for Asbury University in Wilmore, Kentucky and is editor of all music publications for The Salvation Army in Atlanta, Georgia.

Curnow was most recently honored with a listing in the *Grove Dictionary of American Musicians*.

NEXUS
For Solo Trumpet, Winds, and Percussion*

JAMES CURNOW (ASCAP)

NEXUS
For Solo Trumpet, Winds, and Percussion*

JAMES CURNOW (ASCAP)

NEXUS
For Solo Trumpet, Winds, and Percussion

Bb TRUMPET SOLO

JAMES CURNOW

Pedal harmonically